Great and Joyful celebrations at the end of the year

Powerful blessing Prayers

We give thanks to you, O Lord God, we give thanks to you

By Apostle Josephine Ujunma holm

Table of Contents

Introduction

Today we have to enter into covenant and agreement with
the **holy God of** Israel, by accepting the **Lord Jesus Christ,** as our lord
and savior, to help us secure the **blessings,** the miracles, the wonders
and the **great** things from all the satanic dangerous attack of every
wicked one of satan and the **great** power and strength of the LORD God
will set us free from all evil of the end of the year, so we can step into
the new year with a rich harvest of every kind of **goodness,**
righteousness, and truth, as in **we pray,** but because of your **great** love I
can come into your house; I can worship in your holy Temple and bow
down to you in reverence. O LORD, our Lord, your **great**ness is seen in
all the world! Your praise reaches up to the heavens. O LORD, you
protect me and save me; your care has made me **great**, and your power
has kept me safe. The LORD lives! Praise my defender! Proclaim
the **great**ness of the God who saves me. **Genesis 12:2**

Section 1: God has given me a great gift
4.

Psalm 4:7

You have given me **great**er joy than those who have abundant harvests of grain and new wine

Psalm 18:14

He shot his arrows and scattered his enemies; **great** bolts of lightning flashed, and they were confused

Psalm 18:35

You have given me your shield of victory. Your right hand supports me; your help has made me **great**

I enter into covenant and agreement with **Psalm 9:1**
 that I must praise the LORD, with all my heart and I must tell of all the wonderful things he has done in my life Every **minute** and **every** moment of the remaining days and nights of this year and forever. In the spirit world and in the physical world. By the power of the blood of the Lord Jesus Christ, with the fire of God. In the name of the Lord Jesus Christ. Amen.

Today I enter into covenant and agreement with **Genesis 12:2-3**
That God makes me a **great** nation and bless me, and make me famous, as I pray that **the Holy God of** Israel. in the name of the Lord Jesus Christ free everything and everyone that belongs to me from every spiritual and physical diabolical assignment
task, **work, job, position, post, commission, exercise, responsibility, duty, mission,**
appointment, undertaking, and **occupation** of Satan and his cohorts, by the consuming fire of Jehovah God. Every **minute** and **every** moment of the remaining days and nights of this year and forever. In the spirit world and in the physical world. By the power of the blood of

the Lord Jesus Christ, with the fire of God. In the name of the Lord
Jesus Christ. Amen.

Today I enter into covenant and agreement with **Genesis 12:2-3**
That God makes me to be a blessing and will bless those who bless me
and curse those who curse me, as I pray that **the Holy God of** Israel. in
the name of the Lord Jesus Christ free me from every spiritual and
physical diabolical operation **campaign**, **movement**,
process, affair, organization, proceeding, procedure, coordination
of Satan and his cohorts, by the consuming fire of Jehovah God. Every
minute and **every** moment of the remaining days and nights of this year
and forever. In the spirit world and in the physical world. By the power
of the blood of the Lord Jesus Christ, with the fire of God. In the name
of the Lord Jesus Christ. Amen.

Today I enter into covenant and agreement with **Genesis 12:2-3**
That God makes me a **great** nation and blesses me and All the families
of the Earth will be blessed through me, as I pray that
the Holy God of Israel. in the name of the Lord Jesus Christ free every
person that belongs to me from every spiritual and physical diabolical
action
**deed, move, act, performance, exercise, achievement, undertaking,
exploit, accomplishment** of Satan and his cohorts, that comes to steal,
kill and destroy, by the consuming fire of Jehovah God. Every **minute**
and **every** moment of the remaining days and nights of this year and
forever. In the spirit world and in the physical world. By the power of
the blood of the Lord Jesus Christ, with the fire of God. In the name of
the Lord Jesus Christ. Amen.

Today I enter into covenant and agreement with Exodus 6:6
 that the LORD GOD rescue me and set me free from every diabolical
slavery of the satanic kingdoms, land, and powers. as I pray that
the Holy God of Israel. in the name of the Lord Jesus Christ free me

from every wicked diabolical agent of satan that is causing problems.
by the consuming fire of Jehovah God. Every **minute** and **every**
moment of the remaining Months: September, October, November, and
December of this year and forever. In the spirit world and in the
physical world. By the power of the blood of the Lord Jesus Christ,
with the fire of God. In the name of the Lord Jesus Christ. Amen.

Today I enter into covenant and agreement with Exodus 6:6
 that the LORD GOD raise with his mighty arm to bring terrible
destruction upon every diabolical satanic kingdoms, land, and powers
and save me
as I pray that **the Holy God of** Israel. in the name of the Lord Jesus
Christ free me from every diabolical opposing assignment of Satanic
god. by the consuming fire of Jehovah God. Every **minute** and **every**
moment of the remaining Months: September, October, November, and
December of this year and forever. In the spirit world and in the
physical world. By the power of the blood of the Lord Jesus Christ,
with the fire of God. In the name of the Lord Jesus Christ. Amen.

Today I enter into covenant and agreement with Exodus 6:7
that the LORD GOD make me and every person in my family his own
people, and be my God.as I see the glorious light of the Good News of
God. as I understand the message about the glory of Christ, who is the
exact likeness of God, as I come in the Name of the Almighty God to
execute judgment against every evil miracle of the mouth of the dragon,
to Perish and die, by the consuming fire of Jehovah God. Every **minute**
and **every** moment of the remaining days and nights of this year and
forever. In the spirit world and in the physical world. By the power of
the blood of the Lord Jesus Christ, with the fire of God. In the name of
the Lord Jesus Christ. Amen

Today I enter into covenant and agreement with Exodus 6:7

that the LORD GOD set me free from every diabolical slavery of the satanic kingdoms, land, and powers, as I come in the Name of the Almighty God to execute judgment against every evil miracle of the beast. to Perish and die, by the consuming fire of Jehovah God. Every **minute** and **every** moment of the remaining days and nights of this year and forever. In the spirit world and in the physical world. By the power of the blood of the Lord Jesus Christ, with the fire of God. In the name of the Lord Jesus Christ. Amen

Today I enter into covenant and agreement with Exodus 18:10
 That I Praise the LORD, who saved me from all the Devil's evil spiritual satanic diabolical kings and queens **of the whole universe** as I come in the Name of the Almighty God to execute judgment against every evil miracle of all the satanic prophets. to Perish and die, by the consuming fire of Jehovah God. Every **minute** and **every** moment of the remaining days and nights of this year and forever. In the spirit world and in the physical world. By the power of the blood of the Lord Jesus Christ, with the fire of God. In the name of the Lord Jesus Christ. Amen

Today I enter into covenant and agreement with Exodus 18:10
 That I Praise the LORD, who saved me from all the Devil's evil spiritual people of all **the planet** earth, as I come in the Name of the Almighty God to execute judgment against every evil miracle of the demonic spirits. to Perish and die, by the consuming fire of Jehovah God. Every **minute** and **every** moment of the remaining days and nights of this year and forever. In the spirit world and in the physical world. By the power of the blood of the Lord Jesus Christ, with the fire of God. In the name of the Lord Jesus Christ. Amen

Today I enter into covenant and agreement with Exodus 18:10

That I Praise the LORD, who saved me and his people from all the
Devil's evil spiritual satanic diabolical slavery places of satan, as I come
in the Name of the Almighty God to execute judgment against every
evil miracle of all the rulers of the world. to Perish and die, by the
consuming fire of Jehovah God. Every **minute** and **every** moment of
the remaining days and nights of this year and forever. In the spirit
world and in the physical world. By the power of the blood of the Lord
Jesus Christ, with the fire of God. In the name of the Lord Jesus Christ.
Amen

Today I enter into covenant and agreement with Exodus 18:11
that now I know that the LORD is greater than all the Devil's evil
spiritual satanic diabolical gods **of the whole universe**, as I ask the God
of heaven; bring all my glory out of all diabolical attacks of
the end of this year, by the consuming fire of Jehovah God. Every
minute and **every** moment of the remaining days and nights of this year
and forever. In the spirit world and in the physical world. By the power
of the blood of the Lord Jesus Christ, with the fire of God. In the name
of the Lord Jesus Christ. Amen

Today I enter into covenant and agreement with Exodus 18:11
that now I know that the LORD is greater than all the Devil's evil
spiritual satanic diabolical gods **of** all **the planet** earth, as I ask the God
of heaven; bring my greatness out of all diabolical attacks of
the end of this year, by the consuming fire of Jehovah God. Every
minute and **every** moment of the remaining days and nights of this year
and forever. In the spirit world and in the physical world. By the power
of the blood of the Lord Jesus Christ, with the fire of God. In the name
of the Lord Jesus Christ. Amen
This week I enter into covenant and agreement with Exodus 13:21
That the LORD is going before me in a pillar of cloud by day to lead
me on the right way, and in a pillar of fire by night to give me light, that

i might travel by day and by night, without any form of satanic attacks of accident, **crash**, collision,

misfortune,

disaster, **tragedy, setback, calamity, mishap, misadventure at** the end of this year, by the consuming fire of Jehovah God. Every **minute** and **every** moment of the remaining days and nights of this year in the spirit world and in the physical world. By the power of the blood of the Lord Jesus Christ, with the fire of God. In the name of the Lord Jesus Christ. Amen

This week I enter into covenant and agreement with Exodus 13:21
 That the LORD is going before me in a pillar of cloud by day to lead me on the right way, and in a pillar of fire by night to give me light, that i might travel by day and by night, without any form of satanic attacks of Mishap, **accident, disaster, misfortune,**

bad luck, adversity, calamity, at the end of this year by the consuming fire of Jehovah God. Every **minute** and **every** moment of the remaining days and nights of this year and forever. In the spirit world and in the physical world. By the power of the blood of the Lord Jesus Christ, with the fire of God. In the name of the Lord Jesus Christ. Amen

This week I enter into covenant and agreement with Psalms 91:11 that **Jehovah God, in the mighty name of the Lord Jesus Christ** put his angels in charge of me to protect me wherever I go from **all the Devil's evil spiritual satanic diabolical accidents, dangers, Threats and destructions of every evil *transportation of satan i*n** the land, on the water, and on the air **at** the end of this year, by the consuming fire of Jehovah God. Every **minute** and **every** moment of the remaining days and nights of this year and forever. In the spirit world and in the physical world. By the power of the blood of the Lord Jesus Christ, with the fire of God. In the name of the Lord Jesus Christ. Amen

This week I enter into covenant and agreement with Psalms 91:11 that **Jehovah God, in the mighty name of the Lord Jesus Christ** put his angels in charge of me to protect the life of me as I travel by cars,

vehicles, buses, trains, land, roadways, *Highways* airports,
airplanes, airways, waterways, *places* at the end of this year by the
consuming fire of Jehovah God. Every **minute** and **every** moment of
the remaining days and nights of this year and forever. In the spirit
world and in the physical world. By the power of the blood of the Lord
Jesus Christ, with the fire of God. In the name of the Lord Jesus Christ.
Amen

This week I enter into covenant and agreement with Psalms 91:11
that **Jehovah God, in the mighty name of the Lord Jesus Christ**
orders his angels to protect me wherever I go in **the towns, in the
cities, in the villages at** the end of this year by the consuming fire of
Jehovah God. Every **minute** and **every** moment of the remaining days
and nights of this year and forever. In the spirit world and in the
physical world. By the power of the blood of the Lord Jesus Christ,
with the fire of God. In the name of the Lord Jesus Christ. Amen

This week I enter into covenant and agreement with Psalms 91:11
that **Jehovah God, in the mighty name of the Lord Jesus Christ**
commands his angels concerning me to guard me in all my ways from
every wicked diabolical agent of satan and from **Every wicked person
of satan at** the end of this year, by the consuming fire of Jehovah God.
Every **minute** and **every** moment of the remaining days and nights of
this year and forever. In the spirit world and in the physical world. By
the power of the blood of the Lord Jesus Christ, with the fire of God. In
the name of the Lord Jesus Christ. Amen

This week I enter into covenant and agreement with Psalms 91:11
that **Jehovah God, in the mighty name of the Lord Jesus Christ**
commands His angels concerning me to guard me in all my ways. from
all the Devil's evil spiritual satanic diabolical dangers of satan, at
every Crossroad, every roadway, every expressway, every
freeway, every **highway,** every **path,** every **road,** every **route,** every
street at the end of this year, by the consuming fire of Jehovah God.
Every **minute** and **every** moment of the remaining days and nights of
this year and forever. In the spirit world and in the physical world. By

the power of the blood of the Lord Jesus Christ, with the fire of God. In the name of the Lord Jesus Christ. Amen

This week I enter into covenant and agreement with Psalms 91:11 that **Jehovah God, in the mighty name of the Lord Jesus Christ** give his angels orders concerning me, to protect me in all my ways, from **all the Devil's evil spiritual satanic** diabolical dangers of satan at every **roadblock, road map, roadside, roadway, roadworks at** the end of this year, by the consuming fire of Jehovah God. Every **minute** and **every** moment of the remaining days and nights of this year and forever. In the spirit world and in the physical world. By the power of the blood of the Lord Jesus Christ, with the fire of God. In the name of the Lord Jesus Christ. Amen

This week I enter into covenant and agreement with **Leviticus 19:15** **That I** don't pervert justice and I don't show favoritism to the poor or the **great**, but I Judge on the basis of what is right, as I pray in line with Luke 10:19; God has given me authority over all the power of the enemy, and I trample down snakes and scorpions and crush them. Nothing can injure me. Every **minute** and **every** moment of the remaining days and nights of this year and forever. In the spirit world and in the physical world. By the power of the blood of the Lord Jesus Christ, with the fire of God. In the name of the Lord Jesus Christ. Amen

This week I enter into covenant and agreement with Psalm 121:7 The LORD protects me from all evil satanic danger of every enemy and keep me safe, as I pray in line with Psalm 105:1, I give thanks to the LORD as I proclaim his greatness. Every **minute** and **every** moment of the remaining days and nights of this year and forever. In the spirit world and in the physical world. By the power of the blood of the Lord Jesus Christ, with the fire of God. In the name of the Lord Jesus Christ. Amen

This week I enter into covenant and agreement with Exodus 13:21
that The Lord direct me by a pillar of cloud during the daytime and by a
pillar of fire at night, so I can travel either by day or night, as I come in
the authority of Jehovah God with 90.000 billion arrows to strike all the
powers of the enemy to die **at** the end of this year, by the consuming
fire of Jehovah God. Every **minute** and **every** moment of the remaining
days and nights of this year and forever. In the spirit world and in the
physical world. By the power of the blood of the Lord Jesus Christ,
with the fire of God. In the name of the Lord Jesus Christ. Amen
This week I enter into covenant and agreement with **Luke 4:10**
For it is written that the Lord God commands His angels concerning me
to guard me carefully, I come in the authority of Jehovah God, with
90.000 billion arrows to kill all the snakes of the enemy to die **at**
the end of this year, by the consuming fire of Jehovah God. Every
minute and **every** moment of the remaining days and nights of this year
and forever. In the spirit world and in the physical world. By the power
of the blood of the Lord Jesus Christ, with the fire of God. In the name
of the Lord Jesus Christ. Amen

This week I enter into covenant and agreement with **Deuteronomy 31:8**
 That the LORD Himself goes before me to be with me and He will
never leave me or forsake me, so, I do not be afraid or discouraged, I
come in the authority of Jehovah God, with the 90.000 billion arrows to
strike all the scorpions of the enemy to die **at** the end of this year, by
the consuming fire of Jehovah God. Every **minute** and **every** moment
of the remaining days and nights of this year and forever. In the spirit
world and in the physical world. By the power of the blood of the Lord

Jesus Christ, with the fire of God. In the name of the Lord Jesus Christ. Amen

This week I enter into covenant and agreement with **Nehemiah 9:12 that Lord God** lead me with a pillar of cloud by day, and a pillar of fire by night, to light for me the way which i should travel, I lift up my hands towards your Most Holy Place, the Lord, my God. Every **minute** and **every** moment of the remaining days and nights of this year and forever. In the spirit world and in the physical world. By the power of the blood of the Lord Jesus Christ, with the fire of God. In the name of the Lord Jesus Christ. Amen

This week I enter into covenant and agreement with **Psalm 34:7** The angel of the LORD encamps around me who fear Him, and delivers me. I say as it is written in 1 Peter 2:9; I declare the praises of God who called me out of a foundation of wickedness **at** the end of this year, by the consuming fire of Jehovah God. Every **minute** and **every** moment of the remaining days and nights of this year and forever. In the spirit world and in the physical world. By the power of the blood of the Lord Jesus Christ, with the fire of God. In the name of the Lord Jesus Christ. Amen

This week I enter into covenant and agreement with **Psalm 103:20 to say** Bless the LORD for all his angels mighty in strength, who do His word, who hearken to the voice of his command, as I pray as it is written in 1 Peter 2:9; I declare the praises of God who called me out of darkness into his wonderful light. Every **minute** and **every** moment of the remaining days and nights of this year and forever. In the spirit world and in the physical world. By the power of the blood of the Lord Jesus Christ, with the fire of God. In the name of the Lord Jesus Christ. Amen

This week I enter into covenant and agreement with **Psalm 19:13** **that the Lord God** Keep me from deliberate sins and Don't let satanic sins control me. Then I must be free of guilt and innocent of **great** sin, as I pray as it is written in 1 John 5:18; God keeps me safe, and the evil one cannot harm me. by the consuming fire of Jehovah God. Every **minute** and **every** moment of the remaining Months: September, October, November, and December of this year and forever. In the spirit world and in the physical world. By the power of the blood of the Lord Jesus Christ, with the fire of God. In the name of the Lord Jesus Christ. Amen.

This week I enter into covenant and agreement with **Psalm 18:50** **that the Lord God** gives **great** victories to me and shows his unfailing love to me his anointed one and all my descendants forever, as I pray as it is written in Romans 6:14; Sin has no dominion over me since I am not under the law. I am in the grace of God. Every **minute** and **every** moment of the remaining Months: September, October, November, and December of this year and forever. In the spirit world and in the physical world. By the power of the blood of the Lord Jesus Christ, with the fire of God. In the name of the Lord Jesus Christ. Amen.

This week I enter into covenant and agreement with **Psalm 19:11** **that the Lord God** give a **great** reward to me as I obey him, as I praise the Lord God of heaven. Every **minute** and **every** moment of the remaining Months: September, October, November, and December of this year and forever. In the spirit world and in the physical world. By the power of the blood of the Lord Jesus Christ, with the fire of God. In the name of the Lord Jesus Christ. Amen.

This week I enter into covenant and agreement with **Psalm 22:25** **that the Lord God** I must praise you in the **great** assembly and I must fulfill my vows in the presence of those who worship you, so help me Lord, as I pray as it is written in Romans 8:2; The law of the Spirit of life has set me free in Christ Jesus from the law of sin and death. by the consuming fire of Jehovah God. Every **minute** and **every** moment of the remaining Months: September, October, November, and December of this year and forever. In the spirit world and in the physical world. By the power of the blood of the Lord Jesus Christ, with the fire of God. In the name of the Lord Jesus Christ. Amen.

This week I enter into covenant and agreement with **Psalm 21:5 that the Lord God** Your victory brings me **great** honor, and you have clothed me with splendor and majesty, as I pray as it is written in John 8:36; The Son of God has set me free therefore I am free indeed. by the consuming fire of Jehovah God. Every **minute** and **every** moment of the remaining Months: September, October, November, and December of this year and forever. In the spirit world and in the physical world. By the power of the blood of the Lord Jesus Christ, with the fire of God. In the name of the Lord Jesus Christ. Amen.

Section 2: I must shout joyfully to the living God page 13.

Deuteronomy 16:11

Be **joyful** in the LORD's presence, together with your children, your servants, and the Levites, foreigners, orphans, and widows who live in your towns. Do this at the one place of worship

Deuteronomy 16:15

Honor the LORD your God by celebrating this festival for seven days at the one place of worship. Be **joyful**, because the LORD has blessed your harvest and your work

Today I enter into covenant and agreement with Psalm 100
to Shout with joy to the LORD, all the earth, to Worship the LORD with gladness, to Come before him, singing with joy, to Acknowledge that the LORD is God for He made us, and we are his. We are his people, the sheep of his pasture, and I Enter his gates with thanksgiving; I go into his courts with praise, I Give thanks to him and praise his name, For the LORD is good. His unfailing love continues forever, and his faithfulness continues to each generation. **Every minute of** the remaining days and nights of this year and forever. In the spirit world and in the physical world. By the power of the blood of the Lord Jesus Christ, with the fire of God. In the name of the Lord Jesus Christ. Amen.

Today I enter into covenant and agreement with **Deuteronomy 12:12** that I am **joyful** in the presence of God, together with children, my servants, and the people who live in my towns, as I pray as it is written in Psalm 5:12; Surely, LORD, blesses me, the righteous, for God surrounds me with his favor as with a shield. **Every minute of** the remaining days and nights of this year and forever. In the spirit world and in the physical world. By the power of the blood of the Lord Jesus Christ, with the fire of God. In the name of the Lord Jesus Christ. Amen.

Today I enter into covenant and agreement with **Deuteronomy 16:11** That I be **joyful** in the LORD's presence, together with my children, my servants, and my people, the foreigners, the orphans, and the widows who live in my towns, at the one place of worship, as I pray as it is written in 1 Peter 5:7; I cast all my anxiety on God because he cares for me. **Every minute of** the remaining days and nights of this year and forever. In the spirit world and in the physical world. By the power of the blood of the Lord Jesus Christ, with the fire of God. In the name of the Lord Jesus Christ. Amen.

Today I enter into covenant and agreement with **Deuteronomy 16:15** to honor the LORD my God by celebrating at the one place of worship and I am **joyful** because the LORD has blessed my harvest and my hand works, as I pray as it is written in John 14:27; I receive the peace of God, so I do not let my heart be troubled. **Every minute of** the remaining days and nights of this year and forever. In the spirit world and in the physical world. By the power of the blood of the Lord Jesus Christ, with the fire of God. In the name of the Lord Jesus Christ. Amen.

Today I enter into covenant and agreement with **Deuteronomy 28:47** that The LORD blessed me in every way and I must worship God with a glad and **joyful** heart, as I pray as it is written in John 14:27; I receive the peace of God, so I do not be afraid. **Every minute of** the remaining days and nights of this year and forever. In the spirit world and in the physical world. By the power of the blood of the Lord Jesus Christ, with the fire of God. In the name of the Lord Jesus Christ. Amen.

Today I enter into covenant and agreement with **1 Samuel 2:1** The LORD has filled my heart with joy; how happy I am because of what he has done! I laugh at my enemies; how **joyful** I am because God has helped me, as I pray as it is written in Colossians 1:13-14; God has rescued me from the kingdom of darkness and transferred me into the Kingdom of his dear Son, who purchased my freedom and forgave my sins. **Every minute of** the remaining days and nights of this year and forever. In the spirit world and in the physical world. By the power of the blood of the Lord Jesus Christ, with the fire of God. In the name of the Lord Jesus Christ. Amen.

Today I enter into covenant and agreement with **1 Samuel 18:6**

That I be singing **joyful** songs, dancing, and playing tambourines and lyres, as I pray as it is written in Romans 16:20; the God of peace has crushed Satan under my feet, for the grace of our Lord Jesus Christ is with me. **Every minute of** the remaining days and nights of this year and forever. In the spirit world and in the physical world. By the power of the blood of the Lord Jesus Christ, with the fire of God. In the name of the Lord Jesus Christ. Amen.

Today I enter into covenant and agreement with **2 Kings 11:14** the Lord God empowers me to be shouting **joyful**ly and blowing trumpets, as I give thanks to the LORD. **Every minute of** the remaining days and nights of this year and forever. In the spirit world and in the physical world. By the power of the blood of the Lord Jesus Christ, with the fire of God. In the name of the Lord Jesus Christ. Amen.

Today I enter into covenant and agreement with **1 Chronicles 15:16** to sing and to play **joyful** music on harps and cymbals to my God, as I pray as it is written in Ephesians 5:11; I have no fellowship with the unfruitful works of darkness. by the consuming fire of Jehovah God, **every minute of** the remaining days and nights of this year and forever. In the spirit world and in the physical world. By the power of the blood of the Lord Jesus Christ, with the fire of God. In the name of the Lord Jesus Christ. Amen.

Today I enter into covenant and agreement with **2 Chronicles 23:13** that I join all the people to be shouting **joyful**ly and blowing trumpets, as the Temple musicians with their instruments are leading the celebration, as I ask the God of heaven: bring me out of the satanic house of bondage. by the consuming fire of Jehovah God, **every minute of** the remaining days and nights of this year and forever. In the spirit world and in the physical world. By the power of the blood of the Lord Jesus Christ, with the fire of God. In the name of the Lord Jesus Christ. Amen.

Today I enter into covenant and agreement with **Psalm 28:7**
The LORD protects me and defends me as I trust in him. He gives me help and makes me glad; I praise him with **joyful** songs, as I ask the God of heaven: bring me out of the satanic land of bondage. by the consuming fire of Jehovah God, **every minute of** the remaining days and nights of this year and forever. In the spirit world and in the physical world. By the power of the blood of the Lord Jesus Christ, with the fire of God. In the name of the Lord Jesus Christ. Amen.

Today I enter into covenant and agreement with **Psalm 30:11**
that the Lord God has changed my sadness into a **joyful** dance and God has taken away my sorrow and surrounded me with joy, as I ask the God of heaven: bring me out of every kingdom of bondage. by the consuming fire of Jehovah God, **every minute of** the remaining days and nights of this year and forever. In the spirit world and in the physical world. By the power of the blood of the Lord Jesus Christ, with the fire of God. In the name of the Lord Jesus Christ. Amen.

Today I enter into covenant and agreement with **Psalm 40:16**
May all who come to you Lord God be glad and **joyful**. May all who are thankful for your salvation always say, "How great is the LORD, as I ask the God of heaven: declare me innocent and defend my cause against the ungodly. by the consuming fire of Jehovah God, **every minute of** the remaining days and nights of this year and forever. In the spirit world and in the physical world. By the power of the blood of the Lord Jesus Christ, with the fire of God. In the name of the Lord Jesus Christ. Amen.

Today I enter into covenant and agreement with **Psalm 95:2**
to say, let us come before him with thanksgiving and sing **joyful** songs
of praise, as I ask the God of heaven: deliver me from every satanic
lying of wicked satanic people of satan. by the consuming fire of
Jehovah God, **every minute of** the remaining days and nights of this
year and forever. In the spirit world and in the physical world. By the
power of the blood of the Lord Jesus Christ, with the fire of God. In the
name of the Lord Jesus Christ. Amen.

Today I enter into covenant and agreement with **Psalm 149:5**
to rejoice in triumph and sing **joyful**ly all night long, as I apply upon
me the protection power of the blood of the Lord Jesus Christ, with the
Holy fire of God, as I use the protection power of the blood of the Lord
Jesus Christ, with the Holy fire of God, to rescue me from the satanic
activities of every wicked person of this year . by the consuming fire of
Jehovah God, **every minute of** the remaining days and nights of this
year and forever. In the spirit world and in the physical world. By the
power of the blood of the Lord Jesus Christ, with the fire of God. In the
name of the Lord Jesus Christ. Amen.

Today I enter into covenant and agreement with **Jeremiah 31:4**
that the Lord God rebuild me and I take up my tambourines and
dance **joyful**ly, as I cover every area of my life with the power of the
blood of the Lord Jesus Christ, with the Holy fire of God, as I use the
protection power of the blood of the Lord Jesus Christ, with the Holy
fire of God, to rescue everything that belongs to me from the satanic
powers and kingdoms of this year . by the consuming fire of Jehovah
God, **every minute of** the remaining days and nights of this year and
forever. In the spirit world and in the physical world. By the power of
the blood of the Lord Jesus Christ, with the fire of God. In the name of
the Lord Jesus Christ. Amen.

Today I enter into covenant and agreement with **Joel 2:21**

that I don't be afraid, but I be **joyful** and glad because of all
the LORD has done for me, as I ask; O God of Heaven, plead my case
against every ungodly nation of this year. by the consuming fire of
Jehovah God, **every minute of** the remaining days and nights of this
year and forever. In the spirit world and in the physical world. By the
power of the blood of the Lord Jesus Christ, with the fire of God. In the
name of the Lord Jesus Christ. Amen.

Today I enter into covenant and agreement with **Habakkuk 3:18**
that I be **joyful** and glad, because the LORD God is my savior, I ask; O
God of Heaven, rescue me from the deceitful and unjust people of this
year. by the consuming fire of Jehovah God, **every minute of** the
remaining days and nights of this year and forever. In the spirit world
and in the physical world. By the power of the blood of the Lord Jesus
Christ, with the fire of God. In the name of the Lord Jesus Christ.
Amen.

Today I enter into covenant and agreement with **Zephaniah 3:17,**
The LORD my God is with me; his power gives me victory. The LORD
takes delight in me, and in his love, he will give me a new life. He will
sing and be **joyful** over me, as I give thanks to the Lord, by the
consuming fire of Jehovah God, **every minute of** the remaining days
and nights of this year and forever. In the spirit world and in the
physical world. By the power of the blood of the Lord Jesus Christ,
with the fire of God. In the name of the Lord Jesus Christ. Amen.

Today I enter into covenant and agreement with **Romans 12:12**
that I Let my hope keep me **joyful**, as I ask the God of heaven; deliver
me from the power of wicked people. by the consuming fire of Jehovah
God, **every minute of** the remaining days and nights of this year and
forever. In the spirit world and in the physical world. By the power of

the blood of the Lord Jesus Christ, with the fire of God. In the name of the Lord Jesus Christ. Amen.

Today I enter into covenant and agreement with **Philippians 3:1** that I be **joyful** in my union with the Lord, I ask the God of heaven; deliver me from every street accident. by the consuming fire of Jehovah God, **every minute of** the remaining days and nights of this year and forever. In the spirit world and in the physical world. By the power of the blood of the Lord Jesus Christ, with the fire of God. In the name of the Lord Jesus Christ. Amen.

Today I enter into covenant and agreement with **Philippians 4:4** May I always be **joyful** in my union with the Lord. I say it again, as I ask the LORD, my God; take away all sickness from me. by the consuming fire of Jehovah God, **every minute of** the remaining days and nights of this year and forever. In the spirit world and in the physical world. By the power of the blood of the Lord Jesus Christ, with the fire of God. In the name of the Lord Jesus Christ. Amen.

Today I enter into covenant and agreement with **1 Thessalonians 5:16** that I am **joyful** always, as I ask the LORD, my God; take away all miscarriages from me. by the consuming fire of Jehovah God, **every minute of** the remaining days and nights of this year and forever. In the spirit world and in the physical world. By the power of the blood of the Lord Jesus Christ, with the fire of God. In the name of the Lord Jesus Christ. Amen.

Today I enter into covenant and agreement with **Hebrews 12:23**
that I have come to the **joyful** gathering of God's first-born, whose
names are written in heaven and I have come to God, who is the judge
of all people, and to the spirits of good people made perfect, as I ask the
God of heaven; keep me safe from every car accident.by the consuming
fire of Jehovah God, **every minute of** the remaining days and nights of
this year and forever. In the spirit world and in the physical world. By
the power of the blood of the Lord Jesus Christ, with the fire of God. In
the name of the Lord Jesus Christ. Amen.

Today I enter into covenant and agreement with **Jude 1:24**
that the Lord God is able to keep me from falling and to bring me
faultless and **joyful** before his glorious presence, as I ask the God of
heaven; protect me from every motor accident. by the consuming fire of
Jehovah God, **every minute of** the remaining days and nights of this
year and forever. In the spirit world and in the physical world. By the
power of the blood of the Lord Jesus Christ, with the fire of God. In the
name of the Lord Jesus Christ. Amen.

Today I enter into covenant and agreement with **Psalm 5:11**
that the Lord God let me sing **joyful** praises forever and Spread your
protection over me, that all who love your name may be filled with joy,
as I ask the God of heaven; preserve me from every car accident. by the
consuming fire of Jehovah God, **every minute of** the remaining days
and nights of this year and forever. In the spirit world and in the
physical world. By the power of the blood of the Lord Jesus Christ,
with the fire of God. In the name of the Lord Jesus Christ. Amen.

Today I enter into covenant and agreement with **Psalm 30:11**
 that the Lord God has turned my mourning into **joyful** dancing and
the Lord has taken away my clothes of mourning and clothed me with
joy, as I ask the God of heaven; deliver me from every road accident. by
the consuming fire of Jehovah God, **every minute of** the remaining

days and nights of this year and forever. In the spirit world and in the physical world. By the power of the blood of the Lord Jesus Christ, with the fire of God. In the name of the Lord Jesus Christ. Amen.

Today I enter into covenant and agreement with **Psalm 47:1**
that I Clap my hands and Shout to God with **joyful** praise, as I praise the LORD, God of heaven. **every minute of** the remaining days and nights of this year and forever. In the spirit world and in the physical world. By the power of the blood of the Lord Jesus Christ, with the fire of God. In the name of the Lord Jesus Christ. Amen.

Today I enter into covenant and agreement with **Psalm 66:1**
that I Shout joyful praises to God, as I ask the God of heaven; keep me safe from death. by the consuming fire of Jehovah God, **every minute of** the remaining days and nights of this year and forever. In the spirit world and in the physical world. By the power of the blood of the Lord Jesus Christ, with the fire of God. In the name of the Lord Jesus Christ. Amen.

Today I enter into covenant and agreement with **Psalm 84:2**
that I with my whole being, my body, and my soul shout **joyful**ly to the living God, as I ask the God of heaven; rescue me from every crossroad accident. by the consuming fire of Jehovah God, **every minute of** the remaining days and nights of this year and forever. In the spirit world and in the physical world. By the power of the blood of the Lord Jesus Christ, with the fire of God. In the name of the Lord Jesus Christ. Amen.

Today I enter into covenant and agreement with **Psalm 95:1**

that I sing to the L ORD and I shout **joyfully** to the Rock of our salvation, as I ask the God of heaven; rescue every person in my household and me from every plane crash. by the consuming fire of Jehovah God, **every minute of** the remaining days and nights of this year and forever. In the spirit world and in the physical world. By the power of the blood of the Lord Jesus Christ, with the fire of God. In the name of the Lord Jesus Christ. Amen.

Today I enter into covenant and agreement with **Psalm 98:6**
that I make a **joyful** symphony before the L ORD, the King, as I ask the God of heaven; preserve me from every train accident. by the consuming fire of Jehovah God, **every minute of** the remaining days and nights of this year and forever. In the spirit world and in the physical world. By the power of the blood of the Lord Jesus Christ, with the fire of God. In the name of the Lord Jesus Christ. Amen.

Today I enter into covenant and agreement with **Psalm 107:22**
that I offer sacrifices of thanksgiving and sing **joyfully** about the glorious acts of God, as I ask the God of heaven; protect me from every bicycle accident. by the consuming fire of Jehovah God, **every minute of** the remaining days and nights of this year and forever. In the spirit world and in the physical world. By the power of the blood of the Lord Jesus Christ, with the fire of God. In the name of the Lord Jesus Christ. Amen.

Today I enter into covenant and agreement with **Isaiah 54:1**
That I break into loud and **joyful** song I speak, in the name of the Lord Jesus Christ, as I ask the God of heaven; deliver every person in my household and me from every bus accident by the consuming fire of Jehovah God, **every minute of** the remaining days and nights of this year and forever. In the spirit world and in the physical world. By the power of the blood of the Lord Jesus Christ, with the fire of God. In the name of the Lord Jesus Christ. Amen.

Today I enter into covenant and agreement with **Habakkuk 3:18**
 that I must rejoice in the LORD and I must be **joyful** in the God of my salvation, as I say the Lord is the provider for my life as I have seen my enemies defeated by the consuming fire of Jehovah God, **every minute of** the remaining days and nights of this year and forever. In the spirit world and in the physical world. By the power of the blood of the Lord Jesus Christ, with the fire of God. In the name of the Lord Jesus Christ. Amen.

Today I enter into covenant and agreement with **Zephaniah 3:17** that the LORD my God is living among me and God is a mighty savior. He will take delight in me with gladness. With his love, he will calm all my fears. He will rejoice over me with **joyful** songs, as I ask the God of heaven; keep me save by the consuming fire of Jehovah God, **every minute of** the remaining days and nights of this year and forever. In the spirit world and in the physical world. By the power of the blood of the Lord Jesus Christ, with the fire of God. In the name of the Lord Jesus Christ. Amen.

Section 3: Lord Keep me from going the wrong way page 21.

Psalm 25:4
Teach me your **way**s, O LORD; make them known to me

Psalm 17:5
I have always walked in your **way** and have never strayed from it

This Month I enter into covenant and agreement
to pray O LORD, punish those my satanic enemies who say such evil
things against me, as I walk with the compassion and grace of God.
Every minute of Monday, Tuesday, Wednesday, Thursday, Friday,
Saturday, and Sunday of the calendar days and nights of the New Year.
In the spirit world and in the physical world. By the power of the blood
of the Lord Jesus Christ, with the fire of God. In the name of the Lord
Jesus Christ. Amen. **Psalm 109:20**

This Month I enter into covenant and agreement

to pray the way for me to become wise is to honor the LORD; he gives sound judgment to me as I obey his commands for, He is to be praised forever, as I am abounding in the love and faithfulness of God. **Every minute of** Monday, Tuesday, Wednesday, Thursday, Friday, Saturday, and Sunday of the calendar days and nights of the New Year. In the spirit world and in the physical world. By the power of the blood of the Lord Jesus Christ, with the fire of God. In the name of the Lord Jesus Christ. Amen. **Psalm 111:10**

This Month I enter into covenant and agreement
to pray I praise you, O LORD; teach me your **way**s, as I walk with the abundant grace of God. **Every minute of** Monday, Tuesday, Wednesday, Thursday, Friday, Saturday, and Sunday of the calendar days and nights of the New Year. In the spirit world and in the physical world. By the power of the blood of the Lord Jesus Christ, with the fire of God. In the name of the Lord Jesus Christ. Amen. **Psalm 119:12**

This Month I enter into covenant and agreement
to pray O LORD Keep me from going the wrong **way**, and in your goodness teach me your law, as I walk with the great treasure of my heart to bring forth good things. **Every minute of** Monday, Tuesday, Wednesday, Thursday, Friday, Saturday, and Sunday of the calendar days and nights of the New Year. In the spirit world and in the physical world. By the power of the blood of the Lord Jesus Christ, with the fire of God. In the name of the Lord Jesus Christ. Amen. **Psalm 119:29**

This Month I enter into covenant and agreement
 to pray O LORD, remove all my impurity, as I walk abundantly in the loving-kindness and truth of God. **Every minute of** Monday, Tuesday, Wednesday, Thursday, Friday, Saturday, and Sunday of the calendar days and nights of the New Year. In the spirit world and in the physical world. By the power of the blood of the Lord Jesus Christ, with the fire of God. In the name of the Lord Jesus Christ. Amen. **Isaiah 1:25**

This Month I enter into covenant and agreement
_to pray LORD, lead me to do your will daily and make your **way** plain
for me to follow, as my two legs, walk with the authority of the Lord
Jesus Christ to command Satan and his cohorts, that comes to steal, kill
and destroy to fall to their own destruction. **Every minute of** Monday,
Tuesday, Wednesday, Thursday, Friday, Saturday, and Sunday of the
calendar days and nights of the New Year. In the spirit world and in the
physical world. By the power of the blood of the Lord Jesus Christ,
with the fire of God. In the name of the Lord Jesus Christ. Amen **Psalm
5:8**

This Month I enter into covenant and agreement
 to pray LORD, lead me in the right path, O LORD, so that my enemies
will never conquer me and Lord Make your way plain for me to follow,
as I enjoy life in the abundance of God. **Every minute of** Monday,
Tuesday, Wednesday, Thursday, Friday, Saturday, and Sunday of the
calendar days and nights of the New Year. In the spirit world and in the
physical world. By the power of the blood of the Lord Jesus Christ,
with the fire of God. In the name of the Lord Jesus Christ. Amen Psalm
5:8

This Month I enter into covenant and agreement
 to pray Teach me your **ways**, O LORD; make them known to me, as I
come into the abundant blessing of the Gospel of the Lord Jesus Christ.
Every minute of Monday, Tuesday, Wednesday, Thursday, Friday,
Saturday, and Sunday of the calendar days and nights of the New Year.
In the spirit world and in the physical world. By the power of the blood
of the Lord Jesus Christ, with the fire of God. In the name of the Lord
Jesus Christ. Amen **Psalm 25:4**

This Month I enter into covenant and agreement

to pray O LORD, leads me the humble in the right **way** and teaches me your will, I enjoy the abundant supplies of God. **Every minute of** Monday, Tuesday, Wednesday, Thursday, Friday, Saturday, and Sunday of the calendar days and nights of the New Year. In the spirit world and in the physical world. By the power of the blood of the Lord Jesus Christ, with the fire of God. In the name of the Lord Jesus Christ. Amen **Psalm 25:9**

This Month I enter into covenant and agreement
to pray O LORD, teach me the **way** I should go daily and instruct ne and advise me each day and night, I serve the LORD, my God, with joy and gladness of heart. **Every minute of** Monday, Tuesday, Wednesday, Thursday, Friday, Saturday, and Sunday of the calendar days and nights of the New Year. In the spirit world and in the physical world. By the power of the blood of the Lord Jesus Christ, with the fire of God. In the name of the Lord Jesus Christ. Amen
Psalm 32:8

This Month I enter into covenant and agreement
to pray O LORD, instruct me and teach me in the way I should go each day and night and counsel me with your loving eye on me, as I receive the abundance of God. **Every minute of** Monday, Tuesday, Wednesday, Thursday, Friday, Saturday, and Sunday of the calendar days and nights of the New Year. In the spirit world and in the physical world. By the power of the blood of the Lord Jesus Christ, with the fire of God. In the name of the Lord Jesus Christ. Amen **Psalm 32:8**

This Month I enter into covenant and agreement
to pray O LORD, restores my soul, guides me in the paths of righteousness for the sake of your name, as I drink from the river of God. **Every minute of** Monday, Tuesday, Wednesday, Thursday,

Friday, Saturday, and Sunday of the calendar days and nights of the New Year. In the spirit world and in the physical world. By the power of the blood of the Lord Jesus Christ, with the fire of God. In the name of the Lord Jesus Christ. Amen **Psalm 23:3**

This Month I enter into covenant and agreement
to pray O LORD, teach me Your way, O LORD, and lead me on a level path, because of my oppressors, as I walk with the seven fruits of the Spirit of God: love, joy, peace, forbearance, kindness, goodness and faithfulness, into. **Every minute of** Monday, Tuesday, Wednesday, Thursday, Friday, Saturday, and Sunday of the calendar days and nights of the New Year. In the spirit world and in the physical world. By the power of the blood of the Lord Jesus Christ, with the fire of God. In the name of the Lord Jesus Christ. Amen **Psalm 27:11**

This Month I enter into covenant and agreement
to pray O LORD, guide me with Your counsel daily, as I live in the goodness of the Lord because I have become the righteousness of God through Christ Jesus. **Every minute of** Monday, Tuesday, Wednesday, Thursday, Friday, Saturday, and Sunday of the calendar days and nights of the New Year. In the spirit world and in the physical world. By the power of the blood of the Lord Jesus Christ, with the fire of God. In the name of the Lord Jesus Christ. Amen **Psalm 73:24**

This Month I enter into covenant and agreement
to pray O LORD, teach me for your benefit daily and direct me in the way I should go each day and night, as I know the Holy Scriptures, which are able to make me wise in the salvation through faith in Christ Jesus. **Every minute of** Monday, Tuesday, Wednesday, Thursday, Friday, Saturday, and Sunday of the calendar days and nights of the New Year. In the spirit world and in the physical world. By the power of the blood of the Lord Jesus Christ, with the fire of God. In the

name of the Lord Jesus Christ. Amen **Isaiah 48:17**

This Month I enter into covenant and agreement
 to pray O LORD, let me hear Your loving devotion in the morning, for
I have put my trust in You. Teach me the way I should walk, for to You
I lift up my soul, as I declare that the divine power of God has given me
everything I need for a godly life through my knowledge of God, who
called me by his own glory and goodness. **Every minute of** Monday,
Tuesday, Wednesday, Thursday, Friday, Saturday, and Sunday of the
calendar days and nights of the New Year. In the spirit world and in the
physical world. By the power of the blood of the Lord Jesus Christ,
with the fire of God. In the name of the Lord Jesus Christ. Amen **Psalm
143:8**

This Month I enter into covenant and agreement
 to pray O LORD, empower me to walk wisely, and
Nothing will stand in my **way** daily and I will never stumble, as I walk
with the kindness and love of God, our Savior, into. **Every minute of**
Monday, Tuesday, Wednesday, Thursday, Friday, Saturday, and
Sunday of the calendar days and nights of the New Year. In the spirit
world and in the physical world. By the power of the blood of the Lord
Jesus Christ, with the fire of God. In the name of the Lord Jesus Christ.
Amen
Proverbs **4:12**

This Month I enter into covenant and agreement
 to pray O LORD, help to go safely on your **way** and never even
stumble, as I walk with the compassion of God into. **Every minute of**
Monday, Tuesday, Wednesday, Thursday, Friday, Saturday, and
Sunday of the calendar days and nights of the New Year. In the spirit
world and in the physical world. By the power of the blood of the Lord
Jesus Christ, with the fire of God. In the name of the Lord Jesus Christ.
Amen **Proverbs 3:23**

This Month I enter into covenant and agreement
 to pray that I remember the LORD in everything I do, and Lord will show me the right **way**, as I walk with the great love and faithfulness of God into. **Every minute of** Monday, Tuesday, Wednesday, Thursday, Friday, Saturday, and Sunday of the calendar days and nights of the New Year. In the spirit world and in the physical world. By the power of the blood of the Lord Jesus Christ, with the fire of God. In the name of the Lord Jesus Christ. Amen **Proverbs 3:6**

This Month I enter into covenant and agreement
 to pray O LORD, teach me with your wisdom the right **way** to live, as I come near to God with a sincere heart in order to tell the good news of salvation. **Every minute of** Monday, Tuesday, Wednesday, Thursday, Friday, Saturday, and Sunday of the calendar days and nights of the New Year. In the spirit world and in the physical world. By the power of the blood of the Lord Jesus Christ, with the fire of God. In the name of the Lord Jesus Christ. Amen **Proverbs 4:11**

This Month I enter into covenant and agreement
 to pray O LORD, empower me to walk wisely, and
No one will stand in my **way** daily and I will never stumble, as I am filled with the goodness of God into. **Every minute of** Monday, Tuesday, Wednesday, Thursday, Friday, Saturday, and Sunday of the calendar days and nights of the New Year. In the spirit world and in the physical world. By the power of the blood of the Lord Jesus Christ, with the fire of God. In the name of the Lord Jesus Christ. Amen
Proverbs 4:12

This Month I enter into covenant and agreement
 to pray O LORD, empower me to walk wisely, and
No enemy will stand in my **way** daily and I will never stumble, as I rejoice with a cheerful heart because of all the blessings that

the LORD has given me. **Every minute of** Monday, Tuesday, Wednesday, Thursday, Friday, Saturday, and Sunday of the calendar days and nights of the New Year. In the spirit world and in the physical world. By the power of the blood of the Lord Jesus Christ, with the fire of God. In the name of the Lord Jesus Christ. Amen **Proverbs 4:12**

This Month I enter into covenant and agreement
 to pray O LORD, help me to Keep away from all satanic evil of every enemy from me daily, as I look to the LORD God, in every situation. **Every minute of** Monday, Tuesday, Wednesday, Thursday, Friday, Saturday, and Sunday of the calendar days and nights of the New Year. In the spirit world and in the physical world. By the power of the blood of the Lord Jesus Christ, with the fire of God. In the name of the Lord Jesus Christ. Amen **Proverbs 4:15**

This Month I enter into covenant and agreement
 to pray O LORD, help me to avoid all satanic evil of every enemy from me daily, as I remember the goodness of God's word and the power of God in every situation. **Every minute of** Monday, Tuesday, Wednesday, Thursday, Friday, Saturday, and Sunday of the calendar days and nights of the New Year. In the spirit world and in the physical world. By the power of the blood of the Lord Jesus Christ, with the fire of God. In the name of the Lord Jesus Christ. Amen **Proverbs 4:27**

This Month I enter into covenant and agreement
 to pray O LORD, help me to walk straight ahead and don't let me go one step off the right **way**, as I receive all the goodness, grace and mercy of God unto me. **Every minute of** Monday, Tuesday, Wednesday, Thursday, Friday, Saturday, and Sunday of the calendar days and nights of the New Year. In the spirit world and in the physical

world. By the power of the blood of the Lord Jesus Christ, with the fire of God. In the name of the Lord Jesus Christ. Amen **Proverbs 4:27**

This Month I enter into covenant and agreement
to pray O LORD, don't let me go one step off the right **way** daily, as I declare that the goodness and faithfulness of God follow me, all my days. I live in the Lord's house for the rest of my life, as I receive the greatness and goodness of God. **Every minute of** Monday, Tuesday, Wednesday, Thursday, Friday, Saturday, and Sunday of the calendar days and nights of the New Year. In the spirit world and in the physical world. By the power of the blood of the Lord Jesus Christ, with the fire of God. In the name of the Lord Jesus Christ. Amen **Proverbs 4:27**

This Month I enter into covenant and agreement
to pray O LORD, keep every department of my 2 legs and my feet away from all satanic evil of every enemy daily, as I enjoy having the right persons in my home, by the power of God, into. **Every minute of** Monday, Tuesday, Wednesday, Thursday, Friday, Saturday, and Sunday of the calendar days and nights of the New Year. In the spirit world and in the physical world. By the power of the blood of the Lord Jesus Christ, with the fire of God. In the name of the Lord Jesus Christ. Amen **Proverbs 4:14**

This Month I enter into covenant and agreement
to pray O LORD, help me never to set my foot on the path of the wicked satanic people daily as I walk with the incredible wealth of God's grace and kindness towards me into. **Every minute of** Monday, Tuesday, Wednesday, Thursday, Friday, Saturday, and Sunday of the calendar days and nights of the New Year. In the spirit world and in the physical world. By the power of the blood of the Lord Jesus Christ, with the fire of God. In the name of the Lord Jesus Christ. Amen **Proverbs 4:14**

This Month I enter into covenant and agreement
 to pray O LORD, help me never to walk in the way of the wicked satanic people daily, as I ask our God to enable me to live a life worthy of his call into. **Every minute of** Monday, Tuesday, Wednesday, Thursday, Friday, Saturday, and Sunday of the calendar days and nights of the New Year. In the spirit world and in the physical world. By the power of the blood of the Lord Jesus Christ, with the fire of God. In the name of the Lord Jesus Christ. Amen
Proverbs 4:14

This Month I enter into covenant and agreement
 to pray O LORD, help me to leave the company of ignorant people, and help me to live and Follow the **way** of knowledge daily, and May God give me the power to accomplish all good things into. **Every minute of** Monday, Tuesday, Wednesday, Thursday, Friday, Saturday, and Sunday of the calendar days and nights of the New Year. In the spirit world and in the physical world. By the power of the blood of the Lord Jesus Christ, with the fire of God. In the name of the Lord Jesus Christ. Amen **Proverbs 9:6**

This Month I enter into covenant and agreement
 to pray O LORD, help me to walk the **way** of righteousness daily as I follow the paths of justice, as I see the goodness of the Lord in the land of the living. **Every minute of** Monday, Tuesday, Wednesday, Thursday, Friday, Saturday, and Sunday of the calendar days and nights of the New Year. In the spirit world and in the physical world. By the power of the blood of the Lord Jesus Christ, with the fire of God. In the name of the Lord Jesus Christ. Amen **Proverbs 8:20**

This Month I enter into covenant and agreement
 to pray O LORD, help me to forsake foolishness and help me to live, and help me go in the way of understanding daily, as I see the goodness of the Lord in the land of the living. **Every minute of** Monday,

Tuesday, Wednesday, Thursday, Friday, Saturday, and Sunday of the calendar days and nights of the New Year. In the spirit world and in the physical world. By the power of the blood of the Lord Jesus Christ, with the fire of God. In the name of the Lord Jesus Christ. Amen

Proverbs 9:6

Section 4: The blessing of the Lord in 12 months of the New Year page 28.

Genesis 26:12

Now Isaac sowed seed in the land, and in that very year, he reaped a hundredfold. And the LORD blessed him,

Genesis 26:13

and he became richer and richer until he was exceedingly wealthy.

Deuteronomy 8:18

But remember that it is the LORD your God who gives you the power to gain wealth, in order to confirm His covenant that He swore to your fathers, as it is this day.

Deuteronomy 26:10
And now, behold, I have brought the first fruits of the land that You, O LORD, have given me." Then you are to place the basket before the LORD your God and bow down before Him.

Proverbs 10:22
The blessing of the Lord, it makes truly rich, and He adds no sorrow with it neither does toiling increase it

Today I enter into covenant and agreement
 to pray that the blessing of the LORD brings me wealth, without painful toil for it, as I remember the loving kindness of the Lord. **Every minute of** January, February, March, April, May, June, July, August, September, October, November, and December of the calendar days and nights of the New Year. In the spirit world and in the physical world. By the power of the blood of the Lord Jesus Christ, with the fire of God. In the name of the Lord Jesus Christ. Amen

Today I enter into covenant and agreement
 to pray that the blessing of the LORD makes me rich, and he adds no sorrow with it, as I walk with the multitude of God's loving kindness. **Every minute of** January, February, March, April, May, June, July, August, September, October, November, and December of the calendar days and nights of the New Year. In the spirit world and in the physical world. By the power of the blood of the Lord Jesus Christ, with the fire of God. In the name of the Lord Jesus Christ. Amen

Today I enter into covenant and agreement

to pray that the blessing of the LORD makes me rich, and he adds no sorrow with it, as I receive all the good that the Lord does for me.
Every minute of January, February, March, April, May, June, July, August, September, October, November, and December of the calendar days and nights of the New Year. In the spirit world and in the physical world. By the power of the blood of the Lord Jesus Christ, with the fire of God. In the name of the Lord Jesus Christ. Amen

Today I enter into covenant and agreement
 to pray that the blessing of the LORD enriches me, and He adds no sorrow to it, as I am satisfied with the goodness of the Lord. **Every minute of** January, February, March, April, May, June, July, August, September, October, November, and December of the calendar days and nights of the New Year. In the spirit world and in the physical world. By the power of the blood of the Lord Jesus Christ, with the fire of God. In the name of the Lord Jesus Christ. Amen

Today I enter into covenant and agreement
 to pray that It is the blessing of the LORD that makes me rich, And He adds no sorrow to it, as I am full of the steadfast love of the LORD.
Every minute of January, February, March, April, May, June, July, August, September, October, November, and December of the calendar days and nights of the New Year. In the spirit world and in the physical world. By the power of the blood of the Lord Jesus Christ, with the fire of God. In the name of the Lord Jesus Christ. Amen

Today I enter into covenant and agreement
 to pray that the blessing of the LORD makes *me* rich, And He adds no sorrow with it, as I share the stories of God's wonderful goodness.
Every minute of January, February, March, April, May, June, July, August, September, October, November, and December of the calendar days and nights of the New Year. In the spirit world and in the physical

world. By the power of the blood of the Lord Jesus Christ, with the fire of God. In the name of the Lord Jesus Christ. Amen

Today I enter into covenant and agreement
 to pray that the blessing of the LORD, it makes me rich, and he added no sorrow with it, as I called out to the Lord in my distress. I cried to my God for help. He heard my voice from His temple, and my cry for help reached His ears. **Every minute of** January, February, March, April, May, June, July, August, September, October, November, and December of the calendar days and nights of the New Year. In the spirit world and in the physical world. By the power of the blood of the Lord Jesus Christ, with the fire of God. In the name of the Lord Jesus Christ. Amen

Today I enter into covenant and agreement
 to pray that the LORD's blessing enriches me, and he adds no painful effort to it, as I sing with joy about the righteousness of God. **Every minute of** January, February, March, April, May, June, July, August, September, October, November, and December of the calendar days and nights of the New Year. In the spirit world and in the physical world. By the power of the blood of the Lord Jesus Christ, with the fire of God. In the name of the Lord Jesus Christ. Amen

Today I enter into covenant and agreement
 to pray that the LORD blesses me with riches, and I have nothing to regret, as I receive all the goodness of the LORD. **Every minute of** January, February, March, April, May, June, July, August, September, October, November, and December of the calendar days and nights of the New Year. In the spirit world and in the physical world. By the power of the blood of the Lord Jesus Christ, with the fire of God. In the name of the Lord Jesus Christ. Amen

Today I enter into covenant and agreement

to pray that   It is the LORD's blessing that makes me wealthy, as I walk with the blessings and good things of God. **Every minute of** January, February, March, April, May, June, July, August, September, October, November, and December of the calendar days and nights of the New Year. In the spirit world and in the physical world. By the power of the blood of the Lord Jesus Christ, with the fire of God. In the name of the Lord Jesus Christ. Amen

Today I enter into covenant and agreement
 to pray that The LORD's blessing enriches me, and struggle adds nothing to it, as I give thanks to the Lord for His constant love, LORD, in the goodness of your constant love. In your great compassion turn to me. **Every minute of** January, February, March, April, May, June, July, August, September, October, November, and December of the calendar days and nights of the New Year. In the spirit world and in the physical world. By the power of the blood of the Lord Jesus Christ, with the fire of God. In the name of the Lord Jesus Christ. Amen

Today I enter into covenant and agreement
 to pray that the blessing of the LORD establishes me with wealth, and difficulty does not accompany it, as Jehovah God set me free from **all the Devil's evil spiritual satanic diabolical** hidden prison houses of every enemy. **Every minute of** January, February, March, April, May, June, July, August, September, October, November, and December of the calendar days and nights of the New Year. In the spirit world and in the physical world. By the power of the blood of the Lord Jesus Christ, with the fire of God. In the name of the Lord Jesus Christ. Amen

Today I enter into covenant and agreement
 to pray that the blessing from the LORD makes me rich, and he adds no sorrow to it, as Jehovah God help me to walk into liberty at all times.

Every minute of January, February, March, April, May, June, July, August, September, October, November, and December of the calendar days and nights of the New Year. In the spirit world and in the physical world. By the power of the blood of the Lord Jesus Christ, with the fire of God. In the name of the Lord Jesus Christ. Amen

Today I enter into covenant and agreement
 to pray that The LORD's blessing brings me wealth, and he adds no trouble to it, as Jehovah God set me free from **all the Devil's evil spiritual satanic diabolical** source of all satanic curses of every wicked one of satan. **Every minute of** January, February, March, April, May, June, July, August, September, October, November, and December of the calendar days and nights of the New Year. In the spirit world and in the physical world. By the power of the blood of the Lord Jesus Christ, with the fire of God. In the name of the Lord Jesus Christ. Amen

Today I enter into covenant and agreement
 to pray that the blessing of Lord Jehovah makes me rich and there shall be no sorrow with it, as Jehovah God **rescues** every department of my destiny from **all the Devil's evil spiritual satanic diabolical** prison houses of every wicked one of satan. **Every minute of** January, February, March, April, May, June, July, August, September, October, November, and December of the calendar days and nights of the New Year. In the spirit world and in the physical world. By the power of the blood of the Lord Jesus Christ, with the fire of God. In the name of the Lord Jesus Christ. Amen

Today I enter into covenant and agreement
 to pray that It is the LORD's blessing that makes me rich, and hard work adds nothing evil to it, as Jehovah God empowers me to shine forth at all times. **Every minute of** January, February, March, April, May, June, July, August, September, October, November, and December of the calendar days and nights of the New Year. In the spirit

world and in the physical world. By the power of the blood of the Lord Jesus Christ, with the fire of God. In the name of the Lord Jesus Christ. Amen

Today I enter into covenant and agreement
 to pray that the blessing of the LORD, it makes me rich, and toil added nothing thereto, as Jehovah God remove every satanic barrier between me and the
fulfillment of my destiny at all times. **Every minute of** January, February, March, April, May, June, July, August, September, October, November, and December of the calendar days and nights of the New Year. In the spirit world and in the physical world. By the power of the blood of the Lord Jesus Christ, with the fire of God. In the name of the Lord Jesus Christ. Amen

Today I enter into covenant and agreement
 to pray that It is the blessing of the LORD that makes me rich, And He adds no sorrow to it, as the ways of God are the highways of my life at all times. **Every minute of** January, February, March, April, May, June, July, August, September, October, November, and December of the calendar days and nights of the New Year. In the spirit world and in the physical world. By the power of the blood of the Lord Jesus Christ, with the fire of God. In the name of the Lord Jesus Christ. Amen

Today I enter into covenant and agreement
 to pray that the blessing of the LORD is that which makes me rich, and he adds no sorrow with it, as Jehovah God **rescues** every department of me from the source of my troubles. **Every minute of** January, February, March, April, May, June, July, August, September, October, November, and December of the calendar days and nights of the New Year. In the spirit world and in the physical world. By the power of the blood of the Lord Jesus Christ, with the fire of God. In the name of the Lord Jesus Christ. Amen

Today I enter into covenant and agreement
 to pray that the blessing of the LORD, it makes me rich, and he adds no sorrow with it, as Jehovah God empower me to have more abundantly in
my life at all times. **Every minute of** January, February, March, April, May, June, July, August, September, October, November, and December of the calendar days and nights of the New Year. In the spirit world and in the physical world. By the power of the blood of the Lord Jesus Christ, with the fire of God. In the name of the Lord Jesus Christ. Amen

Today I enter into covenant and agreement
 to pray that the blessing of the LORD, makes me rich, and he adds no sorrow with it, as Jehovah God heal me and deliver me from all the satanic destructions of every wicked diabolical agent of satan. **Every minute of** January, February, March, April, May, June, July, August, September, October, November, and December of the calendar days and nights of the New Year. In the spirit world and in the physical world. By the power of the blood of the Lord Jesus Christ, with the fire of God. In the name of the Lord Jesus Christ. Amen

Today I enter into covenant and agreement
 to pray that the blessing of Jehovah, makes me rich; And he added no sorrow therewith, as Jehovah God brings me out of every distress. **Every minute of** January, February, March, April, May, June, July, August, September, October, November, and December of the calendar days and nights of the New Year. In the spirit world and in the physical world. By the power of the blood of the Lord Jesus Christ, with the fire of God. In the name of the Lord Jesus Christ. Amen

Today I enter into covenant and agreement

to pray that the blessing of the Lord is upon the head of me the righteous; it enriches *me*, and grief of heart shall not be added to *it*, as Jehovah God bring me and all my properties out of all the satanic destructions of every person among the witches and wizards. **Every minute of** January, February, March, April, May, June, July, August, September, October, November, and December of the calendar days and nights of the New Year. In the spirit world and in the physical world. By the power of the blood of the Lord Jesus Christ, with the fire of God. In the name of the Lord Jesus Christ. Amen

Today I enter into covenant and agreement
 to pray that the blessing of the Lord makes me rich and neither shall affliction be joined to them, as Jehovah God **rescues** every department of me from suffering the effect of all the satanic curses. **Every minute of** January, February, March, April, May, June, July, August, September, October, November, and December of the calendar days and nights of the New Year. In the spirit world and in the physical world. By the power of the blood of the Lord Jesus Christ, with the fire of God. In the name of the Lord Jesus Christ. Amen

Today I enter into covenant and agreement
 to pray that the blessing of Jehovah, it makes me rich, and he added no sorrow to it, as Jehovah God remove every satanic curse upon my life. **Every minute of** January, February, March, April, May, June, July, August, September, October, November, and December of the calendar days and nights of the New Year. In the spirit world and in the physical world. By the power of the blood of the Lord Jesus Christ, with the fire of God. In the name of the Lord Jesus Christ. Amen

Today I enter into covenant and agreement
 to pray that the blessing of the LORD, it makes me rich, and he added no sorrow therewith, as Jehovah God remove every satanic handwriting that is against me. **Every minute of** January, February, March, April,

May, June, July, August, September, October, November, and December of the calendar days and nights of the New Year. In the spirit world and in the physical world. By the power of the blood of the Lord Jesus Christ, with the fire of God. In the name of the Lord Jesus Christ. Amen

Today I enter into covenant and agreement
 to pray that the blessing of the LORD, it makes me rich, and he added no sorrow with it, as Jehovah God remove every satanic invisible barrier out of every department of my life. **Every minute of** January, February, March, April, May, June, July, August, September, October, November, and December of the calendar days and nights of the New Year. In the spirit world and in the physical world. By the power of the blood of the Lord Jesus Christ, with the fire of God. In the name of the Lord Jesus Christ. Amen

Today I enter into covenant and agreement
 to pray that the blessing of Jehovah it makes me rich, And He added no grief with it, as Jehovah God rescue every department of me from every satanic invisible pit of satan. **Every minute of** January, February, March, April, May, June, July, August, September, October, November, and December of the calendar days and nights of the New Year. In the spirit world and in the physical world. By the power of the blood of the Lord Jesus Christ, with the fire of God. In the name of the Lord Jesus Christ. Amen

Section 5: Trust in the Lord at the last week and day of this year page 34.

Psalm 18:2
The Lord is my rock and my fortress and my deliverer; My God, my strength, **in** whom I will **trust**; My shield and **the** horn of my salvation, my stronghold.

Psalm 31:1
 In You, O **Lord**, I put my **trust**; Let me never be ashamed; Deliver me **in** Your righteousness.

Psalm 37:3
Trust in the Lord, and do good; Dwell **in the** land, and feed on His faithfulness.

1 Corinthians 15:57
But thanks *be* to God, who gives us the **victory** through our Lord Jesus Christ

Today I **trust in the LORD** with all my heart, as I ask the LORD, my God to guard me against all satanic evil of **every minute of** the last month, the last week, and the last day of this year and forever. In the spirit world and in the physical world. By the power of the blood of the Lord Jesus Christ, with the fire of God. In the name of the Lord Jesus Christ. Amen

Proverbs 3:5-6

Today I put my **trust in the LORD,** as I ask the Lord, my God to lead me away from all the satanic troublemakers **of every minute of** the last month, the last week, and the last day of this year and forever. In the spirit world and in the physical world. By the power of the blood of the Lord Jesus Christ, with the fire of God. In the name of the Lord Jesus Christ. Amen
Genesis 15:6

Today I put my **trust in the LORD** of God of Israel, as I ask the Lord, my God to rescue me from all the evil satanic hunters' traps **of every minute of** the last month, the last week, and the last day of this year and forever. In the spirit world and in the physical world. By the power of the blood of the Lord Jesus Christ, with the fire of God. In the name of the Lord Jesus Christ. Amen **2 Kings 18:5**

Today I Put my **trust in the LORD** my God to help me succeed, as I give thanks to the name of the Lord, my God, **every minute of** the last month, the last week, and the last day of this year and forever. In the spirit world and in the physical world. By the power of the blood of the Lord Jesus Christ, with the fire of God. In the name of the Lord Jesus Christ. Amen
2 Chronicles 20:20

Today I Put my **trust in the Lord** for my victory, as I depend on the Lord, my God **every minute of** the last month, the last week, and the last day of this year and forever. In the spirit world and in the physical world. By the power of the blood of the Lord Jesus Christ, with the fire of God. In the name of the Lord Jesus Christ. Amen
2 Chronicles 20:20

Today I offer **the** right sacrifices to **the LORD,** and I put
my **trust in** him and May I be blessed by the Lord, **every minute of** the
last month, the last week, and the last day of this year and forever. In
the spirit world and in the physical world. By the power of the blood of
the Lord Jesus Christ, with the fire of God. In the name of the Lord
Jesus Christ. Amen
Psalm 4:5

Today I put my *Confidence **in the Lord*** and I **trust in the LORD** for my
safety, as I recover all the **blessings, all** the **good things,**
the **great things for me from all the satanic hands of every wicked**
one of satan, every minute of the last month, the last week, and the
last day of this year and forever. In the spirit world and in the physical
world. By the power of the blood of the Lord Jesus Christ, with the fire
of God. In the name of the Lord Jesus Christ. Amen.
Psalm 11:1

  Today I **trust in the** power of **the LORD** our God, as Jehovah God
remove every satanic affliction out of every department of my life,
every minute of the last month, the last week, and the last day of this
year and forever. In the spirit world and in the physical world. By the
power of the blood of the Lord Jesus Christ, with the fire of God. In the
name of the Lord Jesus Christ. Amen.
Psalm 20:7

Today I **trust in the LORD** Almighty; and because of **the LORD**'s
constant love, I will always be secure, as Jehovah God remove every
demonic oppression out of every department of my life, **every minute**
of the last month, the last week, and the last day of this year and
forever. In the spirit world and in the physical world. By the power of

the blood of the Lord Jesus Christ, with the fire of God. In the name of
the Lord Jesus Christ. Amen.
Psalm 21:7

Today declare me **in**nocent, O **LORD**, because I do what is right and I
trust you completely, as Jehovah God remove all the wicked satanic
strange curse things of satan out of every department of my life, **every
minute of** the last month, the last week, and the last day of this year and
forever. In the spirit world and in the physical world. By the power of
the blood of the Lord Jesus Christ, with the fire of God. In the name of
the Lord Jesus Christ. Amen.
 Psalm 26:1

Today I **Trust in the LORD**. Have faith, do not despair, I
Trust in the LORD, as Jehovah God help me to get rid of all the wicked
satanic strange curse things of satan out of my life, so I live a life of
liberty at all times, **every minute of** the last month, the last week, and
the last day of this year and forever. In the spirit world and in the
physical world. By the power of the blood of the Lord Jesus Christ,
with the fire of God. In the name of the Lord Jesus Christ. Amen.
 Psalm 27:14

Today **the LORD** protects me and defends me and I **trust in** him for The
Lord gives me help and makes me glad and I praise him with joyful
songs, as Jehovah God root out the source of all the evil satanic smoke
of fire out of every department of my life, **every minute of** the last
month, the last week, and the last day of this year and forever. In the
spirit world and in the physical world. By the power of the blood of the
Lord Jesus Christ, with the fire of God. In the name of the Lord Jesus
Christ. Amen.
 Psalm 28:7

Today I **Trust in the LORD** and do good and I live **in the** land and be
safe, as Jehovah God help me to enjoy true liberty at all times, **every
minute of** the last month, the last week, and the last day of this year and

forever. In the spirit world and in the physical world. By the power of the blood of the Lord Jesus Christ, with the fire of God. In the name of the Lord Jesus Christ. Amen. **Psalm 37:3**

Today I give myself to **the LORD; trust in** him, and he will help me, as Jehovah God empower me to enjoy the refreshing blessings that comes from heaven, for it's my birthright at all times, **every minute of** the last month, the last week, and the last day of this year and forever. In the spirit world and in the physical world. By the power of the blood of the Lord Jesus Christ, with the fire of God. In the name of the Lord Jesus Christ. Amen. **Psalm 37:5**

Today I **trust in the LORD** to possess **the** land, but **the** wicked will be driven out, as Jehovah God remove all the wicked satanic curses that are choking my life out of every department of my life, **every minute of** the last month, the last week, and the last day of this year and forever. In the spirit world and in the physical world. By the power of the blood of the Lord Jesus Christ, with the fire of God. In the name of the Lord Jesus Christ. Amen. **Psalm 37:9**

Today I sing a new song of praise to our God and will I put **trust in the LORD**, as Jehovah God of vengeance put to death **all the Devil's evil spiritual satanic diabolical** hand of every wicked diabolical agent of satan on my life to die forever , **every minute of** the last month, the last week, and the last day of this year and forever. In the spirit world and in the physical world. By the power of the blood of the Lord Jesus Christ, with the fire of God. In the name of the Lord Jesus Christ. Amen. **Psalm 40:3**

Today I **Trust in the LORD** and He helps me and protects me, as Jehovah God of vengeance put to death **all the Devil's evil spiritual satanic diabolical** hand of every wicked person of satan on my life to die forever, **every minute of** the last month, the last week, and the last day of this year and forever. In the spirit world and in the physical world. By the power of the blood of the Lord Jesus Christ, with the fire of God. In the name of the Lord Jesus Christ. Amen. **Psalm 115:9**

Today I **trust in the LORD** to be like Mount Zion, which can never be shaken, and never be moved, as Jehovah God of vengeance put to death **all the Devil's evil spiritual satanic diabolical** hand of the wicked satanic people of my household on my life to die forever**, every minute of** the last month, the last week, and the last day of this year and forever. In the spirit world and in the physical world. By the power of the blood of the Lord Jesus Christ, with the fire of God. In the name of the Lord Jesus Christ. Amen. **Psalm 125:1**

Today I wait eagerly for **the LORD's** help, and **in** his word, I **trust**, as Jehovah God empowers me to never give place to the devil**, every minute of** the last month, the last week, and the last day of this year and forever. In the spirit world and in the physical world. By the power of the blood of the Lord Jesus Christ, with the fire of God. In the name of the Lord Jesus Christ. Amen. **Psalm 130:5**

Today I say thanks be to God who gives me the **victory** through our Lord Jesus Christ, as Jehovah God empowers me to experience his glorious liberty at all times**, every minute of** the last month, the last week, and the last day of this year and forever. In the spirit world and in the physical world. By the power of the blood of the Lord Jesus Christ, with the fire of God. In the name of the Lord Jesus Christ. Amen. **1 Corinthians 15:57**

Today I May the Most High God, who gave me **victory** over my enemies be praised**,** as Jehovah God empower every part of my body, my hands, my legs, my mouth, my eyes, my ears to experience the glorious liberty at all times**, every minute of** the last month, the last week, and the last day of this year and forever. In the spirit world and in the physical world. By the power of the blood of the Lord Jesus Christ, with the fire of God. In the name of the Lord Jesus Christ. Amen. **Genesis 14:20**

Today I Sing to the LORD because he has won a glorious **victory for me,** as Jehovah God empower every part of my building, my house to experience the glorious liberty at all times, **every minute of** the last month, the last week, and the last day of this year and forever. In the spirit world and in the physical world. By the power of the blood of the Lord Jesus Christ, with the fire of God. In the name of the Lord Jesus Christ. Amen.   **Exodus 15:21**

Today I gain honor and **victory** over every satanic king, his army, his chariots, and his drivers, as Jehovah God help to free me from me, so that I can experience the glorious liberty at all times, **every minute of** the last month, the last week, and the last day of this year and forever. In the spirit world and in the physical world. By the power of the blood of the Lord Jesus Christ, with the fire of God. In the name of the Lord Jesus Christ. Amen. **Exodus 14:17**

Today the LORD GOD GO with me, and give me **victory**, as Jehovah God help me to get out of all the satanic prison houses of the satanic curses of life, **every minute of** the last month, the last week, and the last day of this year and forever. In the spirit world and in the physical world. By the power of the blood of the Lord Jesus Christ, with the fire of God. In the name of the Lord Jesus Christ. Amen.   **Exodus 33:14**

Today I do not be afraid of the enemy for The LORD must give me **victory** over every satanic person, over all his satanic people, and over his land, as the ways of God are the highways to give me freedom from every satanic curse of life, **every minute of** the last month, the last week, and the last day of this year and forever. In the spirit world and in the physical world. By the power of the blood of the Lord Jesus Christ, with the fire of God. In the name of the Lord Jesus Christ. Amen. **Numbers 21:34**

Today the LORD my God is going with me to give me **victory,** as Jehovah God help me to get out of all the type of satanic curses of every enemy**, every minute of** the last month, the last week, and the last day of this year and forever. In the spirit world and in the physical world. By the power of the blood of the Lord Jesus Christ, with the fire of God. In the name of the Lord Jesus Christ. Amen.   **Deuteronomy 20:4**

Today **I** Keep my camp ritually clean, because the LORD my God is with me in my camp to protect me and to give me **victory** over my enemies, as the ways of God are the highways to give me freedom from the curse of God, from the curse of man, from the curse of the law and from the curse of seedtime and harvest at all times, **every minute of** the last month, the last week, and the last day of this year and forever. In the spirit world and in the physical world. By the power of the blood of the Lord Jesus Christ, with the fire of God. In the name of the Lord Jesus Christ. Amen.   **Deuteronomy 23:14**

Today the LORD will give me **victory** over every wicked one of satan, as the ways of God are the highways to give me freedom from the curse of bitterness, from the curse of the prophets and the curse of Satan at all times**, every minute of** the last month, the last week, and the last day of this year and forever. In the spirit world and in the physical world. By the power of the blood of the Lord Jesus Christ, with the fire of God. In the name of the Lord Jesus Christ. Amen.   **Deuteronomy 31:5**

Today the LORD gives me **victory** over every satanic king and queen of universe; his people, city, and land, as Jehovah God, enable me to walk free from the curses of God all the days of my life, **every minute of** the last month, the last week, and the last day of this year and forever. In the spirit world and in the physical world. By the power of the blood of the Lord Jesus Christ, with the fire of God. In the name of the Lord Jesus Christ. Amen.   **Joshua 8:1**

Today the LORD my God has given me **victory** over every satanic king and queen of universe; his people, city, and land, as God is able to make all grace abound toward me at all times, **every minute of** the last month, the last week, and the last day of this year and forever. In the spirit world and in the physical world. By the power of the blood of the Lord Jesus Christ, with the fire of God. In the name of the Lord Jesus Christ. Amen.   **Joshua 10:19**

Today The LORD has given me **victory** over all my satanic enemies, as put my hands into the hands of the Most High God, so no limit to the height I must attain at all times, **every minute of** the last month, the last week, and the last day of this year and forever. In the spirit world and in the physical world. By the power of the blood of the Lord Jesus Christ, with the fire of God. In the name of the Lord Jesus Christ. Amen.
Judges 3:28

Today the LORD is giving me **victory** over all the satanic army of all my satanic enemies, as Jehovah God remove all the satanic curses of limitations that have placed over my life at all times, **every minute of** the last month, the last week, and the last day of this year and forever. In the spirit world and in the physical world. By the power of the blood of the Lord Jesus Christ, with the fire of God. In the name of the Lord Jesus Christ. Amen.
Judges 7:15

Today the LORD won a great **victory** for me, as Jehovah God help me to escape every dagger of curse of God at all times, **every minute of** the last month, the last week, and the last day of this year and forever. In the spirit world and in the physical world. By the power of the blood of the Lord Jesus Christ, with the fire of God. In the name of the Lord Jesus Christ. Amen.

1 Samuel 19:5

Job 22:12

God is so **great**—higher than the heavens, higher than the farthest stars.

Job 36:26

Look, God is **great**er than we can understand. His years cannot be counted.

Job 37:5

God's voice is glorious in the thunder. We can't even imagine the **great**ness of his power.

Psalm 31:19

How **great** is the goodness you have stored up for those who fear you. You lavish it on those who come to you for protection, blessing them before the watching world.

Psalm 34:3

Come, let us tell of the LORD's **great**ness; let us exalt his name together.

Psalm 35:18

Then I will thank you in front of the **great** assembly. I will praise you before all the people.

Psalm 35:27

But give **great** joy to those who came to my defense. Let them continually say, "**Great** is the L ORD, who delights in blessing his servant with peace!"

Psalm 40:10

I have not kept the good news of your justice hidden in my heart; I have talked about your faithfulness and saving power. I have told everyone in the **great** assembly of your unfailing love and faithfulness.

Psalm 20:6

Now I know that the L ORD rescues his anointed king. He will answer him from his holy heaven and rescue him by his **great** power.

Psalm 19:5

It bursts forth like a radiant bridegroom after his wedding. It rejoices like a **great** athlete eager to run the race.

Psalm 40:16

But may all who search for you be filled with joy and gladness in you. May those who love your salvation repeatedly shout,
"The L ORD is **great**

Psalm 42:4

My heart is breaking as I remember how it used to be: I walked among the crowds of worshipers, leading a **great** procession to the house of God, singing for joy and giving thanks amid the sound of
a **great** celebration!

Psalm 47:2

For the L ORD Most High is awesome. He is the **great** King of all the earth.

Psalm 48:1

How **great** is the L ORD, how deserving of praise, in the city of our God, which sits on his holy mountain!

Psalm 48:2

It is high and magnificent; the whole earth rejoices to see it! Mount Zion, the holy mountain, is the city of the **great** King!

Psalm 49:6

They trust in their wealth and boast of **great** riches.

Psalm 50:3

Our God approaches, and he is not silent. Fire devours everything in his way, and a **great** storm rages around him.

Psalm 51:1

Have mercy on me, O God, because of your unfailing love. Because of your **great** compassion, blot out the stain of my sins.

Psalm 54:1

Come with **great** power, O God, and rescue me! Defend me with your might.

Psalm 66:7

For by his **great** power he rules forever. He watches every movement of the nations; let no rebel rise in defiance. Interlude

Psalm 66:12

Then you put a leader over us. We went through fire and flood, but you brought us to a place of **great** abundance.

Psalm 68:11

The Lord gives the word, and a **great** army brings good news.

Psalm 68:27

Look, the little tribe of Benjamin leads the way. Then comes a **great** throng of rulers from Judah and all the rulers of Zebulun and Naphtali.

Psalm 70:4

But may all who search for you be filled with joy and gladness in you. May those who love your salvation repeatedly shout, "God is **great**!"

Psalm 71:21

You will restore me to even **great**er honor and comfort me once again.

Psalm 76:1

God is honored in Judah; his name is **great** in Israel.

Psalm 76:7

No wonder you are **great**ly feared! Who can stand before you when your anger explodes?

Psalm 77:14

You are the God of **great** wonders! You demonstrate your awesome power among the nations.

Psalm 78:11

They forgot what he had done— the **great** wonders he had shown them,

Psalm 79:11

Listen to the moaning of the prisoners. Demonstrate your **great** power by saving those condemned to die.

Psalm 79:13

Then we are your people, the sheep of your pasture will thank you forever and ever, praising your **great**ness from generation to generation.

Psalm 86:10

For you are **great** and perform wonderful deeds. You alone are God.

Psalm 86:13

your love for me is very **great**. You have rescued me from the depths of death.

Psalm 89:5

All heaven will praise your **great** wonders, LORD; myriads of angels will praise you for your faithfulness.

Psalm 89:10

You crushed the **great** sea monster. You scattered your enemies with your mighty arm.

Psalm 92:5

O LORD, what **great** works you do! And how deep are your thoughts?

Psalm 95:3

For the LORD is a **great** God, a **great** King above all gods.

Psalm 96:4

Great is the LORD! He is most worthy of praise! He is to be feared above all gods.

Psalm 99:3

Let them praise your **great** and awesome name. Your name is holy!
Psalm 103:11
For his unfailing love toward those who fear him is as **great** as the height of the heavens above the earth.
Psalm 104:1
Let all that I am praise the LORD. O LORD my God, how **great** you are! You are robed with honor and majesty.
Psalm 105:1
Give thanks to the LORD and proclaim his **great**ness. Let the whole world know what he has done.
Psalm 105:38
Egypt was glad when they were gone, for they feared them **great**ly.

Psalm 105:39
The LORD spread a cloud above them as a covering and gave them a **great** fire to light the darkness.

Psalm 106:21
They forgot God, their savior, who had done such **great** things in Egypt
Psalm 107:8
Let them praise the LORD for his **great** love and for the wonderful things he has done for them.
Psalm 107:15
Let them praise the LORD for his **great** love and for the wonderful things he has done for them.
Psalm 107:21
Let them praise the LORD for his **great** love and for the wonderful things he has done for them.
Psalm 107:31
Let them praise the LORD for his **great** love and for the wonderful things he has done for them.
Psalm 111:6

He has shown his **great** power to his people by giving them the lands of other nations.

Psalm 115:13

He will bless those who fear the LORD, both **great** and lowly.

Psalm 119:156

LORD, how **great** is your mercy; let me be revived by following your regulations.

Psalm 119:162

I rejoice in your word like one who discovers a **great** treasure.

Psalm 119:165

Those who love your instructions have **great** peace and do not stumble.

Psalm 131:1

LORD, my heart is not proud; my eyes are not haughty. I don't concern myself with matters too **great** or too awesome for me to grasp.

Psalm 135:5

I know the **great**ness of the LORD— that our Lord is **great**er than any other god.

Psalm 135:10

He struck down **great** nations and slaughtered mighty kings—

Psalm 137:6

May my tongue stick to the roof of my mouth if I fail to remember you if I don't make Jerusalem my **great**est joy.

Psalm 138:5

Yes, they will sing about the LORD's ways, for the glory of the LORD is very **great**.

Psalm 138:6

Though the LORD is **great**, he cares for the humble, but he keeps his distance from the proud.

Psalm 139:6

Such knowledge is too wonderful for me, too **great** for me to understand!

Psalm 140:11

Don't let liars prosper here in our land. Cause **great** disasters to fall on the violent.

Psalm 143:5

I remember the days of old. I ponder all your **great** works and think about what you have done.

Psalm 145:3

Great is the LORD! He is most worthy of praise! No one can measure his **great**ness.

Psalm 145:6

Your awe-inspiring deeds will be on every tongue; I will proclaim your **great**ness.

Psalm 147:5

How **great** is our Lord! His power is absolute! His understanding is beyond comprehension!

Psalm 148:13

Let them all praise the name of the LORD. For his name is very **great**; his glory towers over the earth and heaven!

Psalm 150:2

Praise him for his mighty works; praise his unequaled **great**ness!

Job 2:13

Then they sat on the ground with him for seven days and nights. No one said a word to Job, for they saw that his suffering was too **great** for words.

Job 3:14

I would rest with the world's kings and prime ministers; whose **great** buildings now lie in ruins.

Job 5:9

He does **great** things too marvelous to understand. He performs countless miracles.

Job 9:10

He does **great** things too marvelous to understand. He performs countless miracles.

Made in Denmark.
By Zion, The City of God

8. November 2019